Tom The Mighty Explorer

by Tim Foley

All rights reserved.
Copyright ©2020 Tim Foley

First published in Great Britain in 2020 by Keel Foley Publishing

A CIP catalogue record for this publication is available from the British Library.
ISBN 9781527277083

The right of Tim Foley to be identified as the author of the work has been asserted by him in accordance with the Copyright, Designs and Patents Act 1988

An adaptation for children based on the book:
Crean - The Extraordinary Life of an Irish Hero - ISBN 9781999918996
Editing and design by Tim Foley
Formatting by Ademir Kalač
Illustrations by Donna Imarts

Keel Foley Publishing goes to every effort to ensure the use of environmentally friendly papers that are natural, renewable and recyclable products and made from wood grown in sustainable forests.

ᴋFᴩ

'Every child needs a Hero
A picture they can hang on a wall
This hero's name is Tom Crean
And he came from Annascaul'

Dedicated to all the little people. Not just leprechauns, elves and fairies but children too.

Tom The Mighty Explorer

Almost 150 years ago in a small cottage that lay in a small townland called Gortacurraun, in County Kerry in Ireland, was born a baby who would one day grow up to become a mighty explorer.

Tom Crean's birthday was 16th February 1877 and he was the seventh-born child of eleven children. He had 7 brothers, Hugh, Cornelius, Patrick, John, Daniel, Michael and Martin and he had 3 sisters, Mary, Joanna and Catherine. His father Patrick was a farmer and his mother, Catherine, looked after him and his brothers and sisters.

Bringing up and having to feed a large family almost 150 years ago was really hard work for Tom's parents. They were very poor yet had to find money to pay rent to a landlord. It was a time when rich landlords owned much of the land and houses across Ireland.

Tom and his brothers and sisters went to the local school but their parents couldn't afford shoes for the children so they all had to walk in their bare feet and that meant walking over hard stones, pebbles and sometimes mud if there was no soft grass to walk on. Tom and his brothers and sisters grew up speaking Irish and they learned English at school along with other subjects like reading and writing.

There wasn't much time for children to play and a lot of their time was spent helping their parents at home and on the farm. They would all help out with the daily chores and there was lots of work to do on the farm.

For Tom, that meant helping his father in the fields and milking or feeding the few farm animals they had, like a cow or a pig. It was important work because families depended on animals and potato crops for their food. Tom had to leave school at 12-years-old because his father needed more help on the farm.

When Tom was young, Ireland was ruled by Great Britain and many of its people were left so poor they felt they had to leave and go to other countries to have a chance of a better life.

Tom's family would earn some money from selling grains, milk or animals but it was wasn't much and those families who couldn't afford to pay the rent were forced to leave their homes.

Tom didn't want this for his family and he'd seen what had happened to other families who were made to leave their homes. Families who were left with no money to pay the rent were removed from their homes by the landlords who owned their houses and the fields on which they farmed. Kindly neighbours would help them out as best they could but homes were too small for one family to live in, never mind two.

Tom knew others who had left Annascaul to

become sailors in the British Navy and the money they earned, even though it was a small amount, helped their families to be able to stay in their homes.

One day, when Tom was meant to be looking after the cows, a gate to the potato field was left open and the cows wandered in. For the cows it was a lovely treat to eat potatoes instead of grass but Tom's father Patrick wasn't happy. The family needed the potatoes for their own food and to sell some at the market. They couldn't sell any after the cows had been chomping at them. Tom's father shouted at him for leaving the gate open. It was Tom's job to make sure it stayed closed.

Upset at being blamed for the cows escaping, Tom, now 16-years-old, decided he had enough of working on the farm. He decided now was the time for him to leave.

He walked down to a nearby beach called Minard where there was a British Navy Coastguard Station. It was a place where boys could go and tell the sailors who worked there that they wanted to join the Navy. It was here that Tom signed to become a sailor on 10th July 1893.

Tom joins the Royal Navy

Joining the Navy meant that he would have to go to England and train to become a proper sailor.

He sailed there on a ship from a place called Cobh in County Cork with his friend James Ashe who was already in the Navy. When they arrived in England they travelled by train to the Navy's dockyard at a place called Devonport on the south coast of England

Tom missed his family and Ireland when he left for England and he would train to be a sailor on a ship called *HMS Impregnable. HMS* stands for *Her Majesty's Ship* and all ships in the British Navy, even today, begin with the letters *HMS*.

It helped Tom a little that other young Irish people had joined at the same time and he would make many friends on the training ship including those from other countries.

Those who trained them were very strict and they often punished the young trainee sailors on board a ship for little or no reason. It was at times like this that Tom wished he had stayed at home in County Kerry but he carried on and was determined to become a sailor.

Young people like Tom would have to learn lots of new things to become real sailors but they also had to continue learning school subjects like Maths and English.

All those training to be sailors lived on the ship and had to sleep in swinging beds called hammocks that were near the bottom of the ship. Hammocks took some getting used to and to begin with Tom would hang on to one side and try to climb into it only to fall to the floor as it swung him upside down.

There were 1500 boys on a ship and it was so dark, cold and uncomfortable that some young people became very ill. Others had to leave the Navy because their trainers believed they would not make good sailors.

Tom's first journey as a real sailor happened in 1894 after his training had finished. It was a time in which Britain ruled over many countries in different parts of the world. This was known as the British Empire and it included countries such as India, Canada, Australia and Ireland.

Tom's first ship journey takes him to America

Being a sailor meant Tom could end up anywhere in the world. His first long journey as a sailor was on board a ship called *HMS Wild Swan* in a voyage which took him a massive 13,000 miles away to South America. He was just 17-years-old. After reaching a South American country called Chile, he joined another ship called *HMS Royal Arthur*, It was the main ship of a fleet of seven ships that watched over the whole West Coast of all of the American continent and lots of islands in the South Pacific Ocean.

When he reached 18-years-old, Tom had become a grown-up in the eyes of the Navy and he was now known as an Ordinary Seaman. This also meant that he was given some extra money in his pay packet.

In the year 1895, Tom's ship, *HMS Royal Arthur* along with *HMS Wild Swan*, and another ship, *HMS Satellite,* were ordered to go on a dangerous mission to get a payment from a South American country called Nicaragua. The Nicaraguans had forced lots of people out of their homes because they saw the area as their own land and they wanted it back.

It was a scary time to be a young sailor and Tom and his shipmates may have had to fight against

Nicaraguan soldiers in a battle to get the money they had come for.

Luckily for Tom, the Nicaraguans paid the money they owed without any fighting and the three ships left the port of Corinto.

Young Tom was beginning to regret joining the Navy but he was able to send the small amount of money he earned back home to his mother and father which helped them keep the farm in Kerry so he knew it was more important for him to continue.

After the trouble in Nicaragua, Tom, rejoined *HMS Wild Swan* and would travel to the main base of the British Navy's Pacific Station, a place called Esquimalt in Canada.

He would spend almost 3½ years on the other side of the world and in that time Tom would visit many other countries such as the United States of America, Mexico, Chile, Peru and Ecuador. He would also travel to many islands in the South Pacific Ocean such as Hawaii, Tahiti and lots of other islands. These places were really hot and Tom and the other sailors were sweating a lot so wore lighter, white uniforms with straw hats.

Not all of these visits were pleasant ones and he saw many battles fought out between people arguing about who would take control of an area.

When Tom's time in the Americas was at an end, the ship returned to England. He carried on with

his learning at lots of training bases before getting on board a ship called *HMS Diana* in the year 1900.

Tom goes to Australia

HMS Diana took him and other sailors out to serve on ships in another part of the world thousands of miles away - Australia. There, Tom would join a ship called *HMS Ringarooma* after arriving in Sydney, a big Australian city.

Tom's time serving with *Ringarooma* was another unhappy time for him and things got off to a bad start when the ship was sent on a mission to stop fighting between groups of local people who lived on many of the islands that are off the coast of Australia.

Even before *Ringarooma* could travel out to the

islands, the ship sailed to a place called New Caledonia where it was kept away from other ships and people. The reason for keeping the ship and her crew away from others was to help stop a disease that could easily be passed on to others if a person caught it. The illness was called The Bubonic Plague and it had already caused the deaths of 103 people in Sydney in the first six months of the year1900.

After it was safe for the ship to leave, *Ringarooma* travelled to visit almost every one of over 80 islands of a place that was then known as the New Hebrides. Today these islands are known as Vanuatu. Tom must have been dizzy travelling to so many different islands.

The ship spent over three months travelling and part of the *Ringarooma's* mission was to help the local people who were fighting one another, to make peace. The job was made much harder because on a few of the islands they visited, the behaviour of some of the people to those they were arguing with was very cruel. Tom and the crew of *Ringarooma* were very upset by what they had seen.

When they returned to Sydney, the crew told newspaper reporters how much they hated the mission they had been on and how it affected them all. A few of the crew decided to run away from the ship. Tom Crean was given a lower rank of 'Able Seaman' just before Christmas in the year 1900 and it could have been that Tom too was unhappy after the mission. It could also have been for something else like arriving back late to the ship after shore leave or for smoking his pipe on the ship when he wasn't supposed to.

A year later in 1901, the man and woman who would one day become the King and Queen of Great Britain, sailed out to Australia as part of their tour to visit the countries of the British Empire. *Ringarooma* would be one of the ships chosen to sail alongside the Royal ship *HMS Ophir* while it was travelling to different cities in the region.

Later in the same year Tom's next journey on *Ringarooma* was to New Zealand.

Tom goes to Antarctica for the first time aboard RRS Discovery

In New Zealand, one of the sailors from another ship called *RRS Discovery* had run away because he knew he would be punished for saying some awful swear words to an officer after an argument. Another sailor was needed to replace him. The *Discovery* was heading to Antarctica to explore the icy continent where very few people had ever been to. The leader of the ship, Commander Robert Scott, chose Tom Crean and Tom left *Ringarooma* to join his new shipmates going to Antarctica. It must have been a bit scary for Tom but he hadn't been happy serving on

missions for the last 6 years and this journey was to a very different place to those he'd already been to.

When they got to Antarctica Tom's job was to pull sledges as members of the crew went out on long journeys across the snow and ice. These journeys were for the scientists in the crew to find out more about the freezing cold land and that's why the ship was called *Discovery*.

Near the centre of Antarctica was a place called the South Pole and no person had ever reached there but many wanted to. For a very short time, Tom, while pulling the sledge with food and supplies, was part of a team of men who had travelled further south than any other people in history. Shortly after though, his Commander, Robert Scott along with two other men, Edward Wilson and Ernest Shackleton, travelled a little further south but they never reached the South Pole and had to turn back because Shackleton became ill.

When it was time for *Discovery* to leave Antarctica she became stuck in the ice and all the crew worked hard to free the ship. They used saws and pick axes to cut through the ice and at one point, with the holes they had opened up, Tom fell into the freezing waters below. Two other crew members pulled him out of the freezing waters and he was shivering, shaking and drenched to the skin. Straight after being pulled out he carried on hacking at the ice only to fall into the water again and ended up freezing and soaked once again. Over the rest of his time in the Navy, Tom Crean would have many similar falls but he was a tough man and he would always carry on as if nothing had happened.

The work of those on the *Discovery* expedition was seen as a great success and there were many new discoveries made by the scientists.

When the ship arrived back to England in September 1904, the expedition leader, Captain Scott, said to his bosses that Tom should be rewarded with a more important position. At 27-years-old, Tom was made a 'Petty Officer First Class' and it made him extremely proud that

someone believed he'd done great work in Antarctica.

In fact Scott, who was now Captain Scott, thought Tom was such a good sailor that he asked for Tom to be with him on all four of the ships he was captain of for the next few years until he made plans to go back to Antarctica.

Shackleton, the man who became ill when Scott was trying to get to the South Pole, went on his own Antarctic expedition on a ship called *Nimrod* in 1907. He wanted to be the first man to reach the South Pole but he never quite made it and again he had to turn back. He did though, reach further south than anyone else had ever done and when he returned to England he was made a knight by the king. Becoming a knight meant that he was now known as Sir Ernest Shackleton.

Captain Scott really wanted to be the first man to get to the South Pole and in 1910 he set off again in a ship called *Terra Nova*. Because he knew how good and how strong a sailor Tom Crean was, Tom was one of Scott's first choices to go to back to Antarctica with him.

What it was like for Tom in Antarctica?

Antarctica is so cold that if you tip a cup of boiling water out it will disappear into freezing mist before it even touches the ground. If you think of the coldest days that you ever went out, then in Antarctica all the days are much, much colder than you can ever imagine. It's colder in Antarctica than it is in the freezer in your home.

In Antarctica not many animals can stand the cold temperatures and those that do spend time there are ones you might have heard of such as, whales, dolphins, penguins and seals. Even though Polar bears can live in the freezing cold, there are no Polar bears in Antarctica.

Almost all of Antarctica is covered in ice and in many places it's over a mile deep. There are many massive holes that go deep underground and often they are hidden under the snow. These holes are called 'crevasses' and lots of people who have been to Antarctica have fallen into them. Tom's friend William Lashly fell into a crevasse on Christmas Day which was his birthday. Luckily he had a rope tied to him and Tom and two other people pulled him out.

There are no places to buy a burger or fries in Antarctica and that's a good thing because too many burgers and fries aren't good for you. So, to keep them fit, healthy and strong, explorers like Tom would eat a food called Hoosh which was made from a mixture of fat, dried meat and hard biscuits which were crushed. All of these were put in a pot, mixed with snow and heated up on a little cooker to make a stew. It may not sound as tasty as a burger and fries but it helped the explorers to build up their strength to pull heavy sledges.

Tom goes back to Antarctica for a second time aboard Terra Nova

This time Scott told everyone that he would try to become the first man to reach the South Pole but there was another explorer from Norway called Roald Amundsen who wanted to do the same.

Lots of Tom's Navy friends who were with him on the earlier expedition aboard the ship *Discovery,* were a part of the new expedition ship which was called *Terra Nova.*

On one of the missions to pull sledges full of supplies to make a depot for explorers to rest at, Tom and two other men called Henry Bowers and Apsley Cherry-Garrard, had to set up their tent on the ice because of a bad blizzard. They had four very tired ponies and two sledges with them. As they rested inside the tent they suddenly heard loud noises. When they looked outside they were shocked to find that the ice they were on had cracked and had broken away from the rest of the ice. They could see the same was happening all around them and they were now floating on a big piece of ice known as an ice-floe. They had to do something very quickly because the ice-floe was floating out to sea and away from Antarctica.

What made things worse was that hungry killer whales were circling in the water around them and popping their heads above the ice looking at the men and the ponies as their next meal.

One of the men had to go and get help but it would be difficult to get across all the large pieces of floating ice to reach the safe ice where the ground was solid. It was decided that Tom would be the right man for the job.

With a long stick in his hand Tom jumped from one ice-floe to another being careful to stay out of the way of the killer whales. He had to reach the safety of the mainland ice and get help because his two friends and the ponies were in great danger as the floes were bobbing up and down and at any time they could fall into the frozen sea beneath them.

Bowers and Cherry-Garrard worried for themselves and for Tom's safety as they watched him jumping from one big piece of floating ice to the next and soon he reached the ice-shelf.

The ice-shelf was the name given to where the mainland of Antarctica rises up from the sea like a cliff. Tom would have to climb it and get to the top where he could travel on the flat ice to try and find help.

Meanwhile on the ice-floes, two of the ponies and a sledge had fell into the freezing waters and were now lost.

Tom rushed to find help and came across Captain Scott and an Army officer who was part of the expedition, a man called Lawrence Oates.

All three men hurried back to where Bowers and Cherry-Garrard were stuck on the ice-floe. They managed to rescue the two stranded men yet just one of the poor ponies survived.

This was the first of Tom Crean's lifesaving acts in Antarctica but he would go on to be as just as brave the next time his help was needed.

Nearly 8 months later Captain Scott and a group of explorers including Tom, set off to reach the South Pole. It was a long, long journey of many hundreds of miles over ice ground called the Ross Ice Shelf. They then had to travel up a massive, sloping ice-valley 125 miles long and surrounded by icy mountains. This was called the Beardsmore Glacier and when they reached the top there was a huge area of ice called the Polar Plateau.

At the centre of the Polar Plateau was the South Pole.

Scott and a team of seven men travelled across the Polar Plateau until they reached close to 150 miles of the South Pole where they set up tents for a rest.

The eight men were Scott, his second in command Lieutenant Edward Evans, Lawrence Oates, Dr Edward Wilson, Henry Bowers, William Lashly, Tom Crean and Tom's best friend on the expedition, a strong Welshman called Edgar Evans.

After their rest, Scott decided that Tom, William Lashly and Lieutenant Evans should return to base almost 800 miles back to where they'd travelled from, a place called Hut Point.

Scott and the other four men travelled on towards the South Pole.

Tom was very upset that he wasn't chosen to go to the South Pole with Scott and tears rolled down his face as he waved his friends goodbye and wished them good luck.

Tom, William Lashly and Edward Evans set off on their journey back to Hut Point on 4th January 1912. They were now pulling a big sledge across the ice that was meant for four men to pull. It was much harder for three to pull it but they worked hard to travel across the ice as quickly as they could.

At one point they walked many miles in the wrong direction and found themselves way off course. The quickest way to get back on track would be to slide down a huge ice slope and back on to the Beardsmore Glacier. It was a dangerous thing to do but they had no choice as their food and fuel supplies were getting low. At certain points across the whole route, other expedition members had left stores of food, fuel and supplies to prepare for the journey to the Pole. These were known as depots. The three men had to reach one soon or they would run out of food and without fuel they would have no way of keeping warm when they stopped for a rest in the tent.

They decided that the risk was worthwhile and they all sat on the sledge and placed their legs each side of one another. They shuffled themselves forward and off they went, whizzing really fast down the ice slope. When they hit a bump in the ice, it would lift the sledge into the air and they were almost flying until they landed back on the ground with a great thud.

It was amazing how they survived but all they had were a few scratches and bruises. Poor Tom's trousers had a hole torn in the backside and the cold and snow was freezing his bottom but he remembered he'd left a spare pair of trousers at the depot and when they reached there he quickly changed into them.

Soon they reached another place of danger. It was a crevasse and the only way they would be able to cross the huge, deep hole was over a bridge of ice that stretched right across it. The massive hole of the crevasse was so deep they couldn't even see the bottom. They knew they would be risking their lives crossing the bridge but they had no choice, it was the only way if they were to make it back to the hut.

William went first. He sat on the ice bridge and he had a rope tied to him which Tom and Lieutenant Evans kept a hold of just in case he slipped and fell. Slowly he made his way across and after what seemed like hours, he reached the other side. Now it was Tom and Teddy Evan's turn but their bridge crossing would be more dangerous because they had to bring the sledge with them.

Tom sat on the bridge backwards as he had to pull the front of the sledge. He shuffled his bottom backwards so that the sledge was on the bridge and Evans sat on so he could push the back end of the sledge each time Tom pulled it forward. The sledge was wider than the bridge so it was leaning to one side and only one of its runners was on the bridge.

William was holding the rope on the other side but he would have had no chance of saving his two friends if they and the sledge slipped off the bridge. Tom shuffled and pulled the sledge while Evans shuffled and pushed until finally they reached the other side. As they hopped off the bridge onto the safe ground, the sledge suddenly dropped into the deep crevasse. Luckily the rope was still tied to it but it took the strength of all three men to pull it back up. When the sledge was back up all three breathed a huge sigh of relief and sat down for a well deserved rest.

As they continued their long journey back, Edward Evans, became ill and was finding it hard to keep up with Tom and William Lashly.

They still had hundreds of miles to travel and on the way back they faced more dangers from frozen winds and more crevasses, even worse if they were hidden under the snow.

Importantly, and even though Evans was still very sick, they managed to pull the sledge to the depots on time but Evans was getting much worse. After reaching One Ton Depot, the main storage depot, they were now 120 miles from Hut Point and the safety and warmth of the expedition's hut.

As Evans condition became more serious, he told Tom and William to carry on without him because he knew that slowing them down would put all their lives in danger. Not reaching the remaining depots at the right time meant they would run out of fuel and food.

Crean and Lashly refused to leave him and Tom said to Evans, *"If anything bad is going to happen to you then it will happen to us too. We are not leaving you."*

Evans was their commanding officer and said later that it was the first time that anyone had refused his orders.

Tom and William decided to put Evans on the sledge. They covered him up to help protect him from the cold winds and they pulled the sledge with all their might across the ice.

After 40 miles of hauling their sick commander on the sledge they reached a place called Corner Camp and here they set up a tent. All three men were absolutely exhausted but Evans was now close to death.

There were still many miles to travel if they were to reach safety. On the morning of 18th February 1912, Evans fainted and Tom leant over him crying because he thought he was dead. As Tom's tears fell on Evans face he opened his eyes and gave a kind of weak laugh. Evans was alive but only just and Tom and William now knew that to have any chance of saving him, one of them must go ahead on their own and try to fetch help.

Tom Crean said he would go even though it was a long distance of 35 miles to the hut. Lashly stayed to look after Evans in the tent and Tom set off on his march through the snow, ice and blizzards at 10 o'clock in the morning. It was a very dangerous journey for Tom and he took

with him two biscuits and a stick of chocolate which he put in his pocket.

After struggling against the freezing winds and trudging through the snow without skis to help him, Tom stopped and sat on the top of a hill for a small rest about half the way back.

He was tired but he knew he had to continue if there was to be any chance of saving the life of Evans.

After almost 18 hours he reached the hut and was completely exhausted as he came through the door out of breath.

Even though Tom was really tired, he told the commanding officer at the hut, Dr. Edward Atkinson, that he wanted to return with him to

rescue his two friends. Atkinson refused and with the dogs pulling the rescue sledges, he and a Russian dog-handler called Dmitry, picked up Evans and Lashly. Evans was still alive when they reached Corner Camp. It was the bravery of Tom Crean and his amazing march of 35 miles in 18 hours on the coldest and windiest place on earth that had saved Evans life.

Very sadly, Captain Scott and his team lost their lives on their own return journey. They did manage to reach the South Pole but the Norwegian Roald Amundsen and his team had already reached there and it was they who became the first humans to plant their country's flag at the South Pole.

Later in 1912, when the crew had long given up hope of Scott and his team being found, Tom Crean, while searching for Scott and his team, spotted a tent through the mist just a few miles past One Ton Depot. Inside were the bodies of Scott, Henry Bowers and Dr. Wilson. Scott had by his side a diary that revealed how the other two men, Tom's great friend, Edgar Evans and Lawrence Oates had died. Everyone was extremely upset that their friends didn't make it back safe. Tom cried and remembering Scott he said: *"I loved that man."*

A few months later in the following year, 1913, the crew left Antarctica and headed home. They sailed into Cardiff in Wales and because they were without Captain Scott and four other shipmates, they all looked very sad.

For his lifesaving walk to save the life of Edward Evans, Tom Crean was given a special medal for bravery from the King of England. It was called the Albert Medal and only very few, brave people ever received one. Because William Lashly stayed to look after Evans and helped keep him alive, he too was given the same medal.

Tom had proven he was a mighty man but it would not be the last time his bravery would be needed.

Tom goes back to Antarctica but who with? Stackhouse or Shackleton?

Later the same year, a man called Joseph Foster Stackhouse, had told the newspapers he was going to lead an expedition to Antarctica in August 1914. It would be called the British Antarctic Expedition and he was planning to use a ship that Tom Crean knew well from his first expedition to Antarctica - *RRS Discovery. RRS* stands for *Royal Research Ship.*

Stackhouse had heard all about the brave Tom Crean saving the life of Edward Evans and he really wanted to bring the hero, Tom Crean, with him on his expedition. He told the newspapers that Crean's lifesaving walk was one of the bravest things he had ever heard of.

Shortly after, another man told the newspapers that he was going on an expedition to Antarctica at the same time. That man was Sir Ernest Shackleton who Tom had served with on the *Discovery* Expedition. He too wanted to take Tom on his expedition to cross the whole of Antarctica from one coast on the Weddell Sea, to the other coast on the opposite side, the Ross Sea. He would use a ship called *Endurance* and for the Ross Sea party he would use another ship called the *Aurora*.

A team of men from *Aurora* would lay stores from the opposite side of Antarctica so that the team from *Endurance* making the crossing from the other side of Antarctica, wouldn't run short of supplies.

In a later newspaper article Stackhouse reported that Tom was going with his expedition but Stackhouse had to change his plans and start his expedition the following year, 1915. This meant that Shackleton was now free to ask Tom to go with him.

Shackleton's expedition was called the Imperial TransAntarctic Expedition and Tom was made the expedition's Second Officer. It was an important role but Shackleton knew just how important Tom would be to him.

Tom's final expedition to Antarctica aboard Endurance

Endurance left London in August 1914 and headed out to Buenos Aries, the capital city of Argentina. From there the ship travelled closer to Antarctica to an island called South Georgia in the South Atlantic Ocean. Not many people lived in South Georgia and those who did worked there as whalers. It was a time when poor whales were hunted and killed for their oil and other parts such as their baleen, the strong filters in a whale's mouth which it used to capture fish. The baleen was used for ladies fashion but thankfully today this doesn't happen and whales are protected.

From South Georgia the *Endurance* set out for Antarctica but soon the ship became stuck in the thick sea-ice. Tom and the rest of the crew tried to free the ship with big saws but no matter how hard they worked they couldn't free *Endurance*.

While the ship was stuck in the ice, the crew found time to entertain themselves and one of the things they did was to play football on the ice. It was really funny to watch as the two teams would slip and slide and fall to the ground as they chased after the ball. Being big and strong and not wanting to be on the losing team, Tom would stop other players scoring in his goals by grabbing them and wrestling them to the ground. While they were on the ground he would sit on them so they couldn't join in the game again while a player from his own team would then be free to score a goal. It was a little naughty and he would be sent off if he did it in a proper football match back home, but the others saw it as harmless fun and Tom's team always won.

After all the fun and games they just couldn't free the ship from the ice no matter how hard they tried and soon the time came for them to leave the ship before it sank. Their plans to cross Antarctica were now at an end and they now had a new mission, to save themselves.

They took all the stores and food supplies they would need from the ship and loaded them into three smaller lifeboats that were on the ship.

The three boats all had names. The smallest was called the *Stancomb Wills* and there was the *Dudley Docker* and the largest of the three was called the *James Caird*. They were named after people who had given Shackleton money to help to pay for their expedition.

Now they would have to drag the three boats across the ice until they could find somewhere they could put them in the sea. When they did find a place they could then row somewhere safer away from the floating ice beneath them.

The crews dragged the boats with their harnesses attached to their waists but it was hard work with all the bumps, hills and ripples on the ice.

They had to stop and put up the tents for long periods of rest and to help stock up on stores that were still on the ship, some of the men would travel back to pick them up. They would attach the dogs to a sledge to make the journeys back to their sinking ship.

The men gave names to the places they stopped at, places such as *Ocean Camp* and *Patience Camp*.

Some time later they looked back to see the ship break up and sink under the ice.

On *Endurance* they had brought with them many dogs as they knew they would have needed them for pulling sledges across the ice. The crew became very close to the dogs and Tom's

favourite was called Sally. In Antarctica, Sally became the mother of four beautiful, cuddly puppies and Tom became like their proud father. They were called Roger, Nell, Toby and Nelson.

Sadly, the time had come when the dogs were no longer needed to pull the sledges and there would be no room for them in the boats if the men were to find open water.

Shackleton, as the leader, had to make a horrible decision to leave the dogs and it upset him and all of the crew. For Tom, it was heartbreaking but he would have no choice. All the dogs, including Sally, her pups and their daddy, a dog called Samson, had to stay behind.

The crew marched on pulling the boats and after

a while they came across a place where they could put the boats into the water and row them. They split into three groups and each group climbed into one of the boats.

Tom took charge of the *Stancomb Wills*, Shackleton was in command of the *James Caird* and Frank Worsley, the person who had been captain of *Endurance* before she sank, took charge of the *Dudley Docker*.

After a week of rowing around icebergs, in rough seas and having to sail through narrow lanes of water, the boats reached a place called Elephant Island. The crew of 28 were tired, cold and hungry. Some of the crew were in a very bad condition – the youngest, a Welshman called

Perce Blackborrow, had terrible, painful toes which had really bad frostbite from the cold.

Elephant Island was a place where no people were able to live. It was too cold, too rocky and too windy to live there. The nearest place they could reach people who might be able to help them was hundred's of miles away and it would have been far too dangerous to try and reach there in three small boats.

The men made a shelter by turning two of the boats upside down so they would be protected from the freezing winds and from the big waves that blasted into the shore.

The carpenter, a man called Harry McNish, would make some important changes to the largest boat the *James Caird*, so that it could be used to get help. He made the sides higher and he put a canvas covering over the top to shelter its crew from the sea. This boat would have to reach a place where they could get help and come back to rescue those men who would have to stay on Elephant Island.

Shackleton, the leader, chose five of the crew to sail with him in the *James Caird* and one of them was Tom. The other four were the Scottish carpenter, Harry McNish, Frank Worsley from New Zealand, Tim McCarthy, another Irish sailor from Kinsale in County Cork and a sailor called John Vincent from Birmingham in England.

On 24th April 1916, which also happened to be

Easter Monday, the *James Caird* lifeboat sailed away from Elephant Island as the 22 men left on the island, waved to their six friends from the shore.

Tom and the other Irishmen in the small lifeboat that day would not have known that back in Ireland, their countrymen and women had on this same day, organised a protest against British Rule in Ireland. It was known as the Easter Rising and it would eventually lead to most of Ireland becoming a nation which ended British rule but very sadly it happened after many lives had been lost.

The *James Caird* sailed though storms and huge waves across the most ferocious ocean on earth, the Southern Ocean.

It was so cold that ice was sticking to the outside of the boat and the crew had to hack it off with hammers in case the boat became too heavy and sank. Even though what was happening outside the boat was frightening for the crew, Tom Crean kept their minds off the terrifying conditions by singing some song that no-one could understand the words to.

Worsley seemed to think it was an old Irish song called 'The Wearing of the Green' but whatever it was it brought a smile to the others when they were in real danger.

After two weeks in the boat the men were tired, wet, cold and hungry. All they had taken to eat

was hoosh, the not so nice mix of fat, dried meat and biscuits mixed with hot water. To cook hoosh on the small camping stove took ages and loose reindeer hair from the sleeping bags above the cooker fell in to the pot to make it taste even worse.

Suddenly they sighted land and had reached South Georgia, the island they had set off from almost a year and a half before. They knew people were on this island yet the whalers lived on the opposite side from where the *James Caird* landed and there was a dangerous mountain range separating the two sides of the island.

The six men were completely exhausted and

set up a camp, they gave this a name too. They called it *Peggoty Camp* and turned the lifeboat upside down to protect them from the cold winds, the snow and the rain.

After nine days rest, it was decided that Shackleton with two of the crew, would try to reach the other side of the island to get some help but it would mean crossing dangerous mountains that no man had ever crossed before. He chose Tom and Frank Worsley to go with him. The other three men would wait to be rescued after the three climbers had reached the whaling station.

After so long a time without a wash or a shave the men looked and smelled awful and they had

torn, wet clothing and long, straggly hair and beards. To help them climb the mountains the carpenter, McNish, fixed nails to poke out of the bottom of their boots so that they wouldn't slip on the icy paths they would have to travel along.

Tom, Shackleton and Frank Worsley tied a long rope around their waists so that all three of them were attached to one another and by the light of the moon they set off into the mountains.

Without a map to show them the way they discovered they had travelled in a circle that led them back to where they had already been and at one point, to take a short cut, they did what Tom had done before when he was with Evans and Lashly on the *Terra Nova* expedition – they slid down an icy slope together. This time they

did it without a sledge and it was frightening as they whizzed down the icy but they survived it with a few bruises and three very sore bottoms.

They were almost a day and a half into their trek when they heard the faint sound of a steam whistle and they knew now that they were near the whaling station at a place called Stromness.

The men followed a snow-covered icy route when Tom suddenly sunk below the snow up into frozen water.

It was only later that they all found out Tom had dropped into a lake and today on South Georgia that lake is named Crean Lake in memory of Tom.

After climbing up to a ridge, the men came

across a waterfall and using their rope they climbed down.

They could now see Stromness and a whaling ship coming into the bay. The three men, looking like scary zombies with their long hair and beards and their ragged clothes, hurried toward Stromness. As they did, two young girls saw them and ran away screaming and frightened for their lives. The same happened with a man they came across until finally they met a Norwegian whaler who took them to the whale station manager's house.

The manager was called Mr Sorle and he knew Shackleton before *Endurance* had set off from the same place a year and a half before. This time though, he didn't have a clue who these three scruffy strangers were standing at his door.

The manager said: *"Who the heck are you?"* They explained and told him of the terrifying journeys they had to make it this far. As they told their story, the manager and a number of whalers wept, imagining the frightening and dangerous experiences they had been through.

After a lovely hot dinner, a bath and a shave, the three men planned their next move. They had to organise a rescue of their 22 crew-mates who were left on Elephant Island. After a wash and a change of clothes Frank Worsley travelled on a whaler's ship to the other side of the island to pick up McNish, McCarthy and Vincent. Worsley looked so different after a shave and a haircut that at first the other three didn't recognise him. He brought them back and they too had a hot meal, a bath and a clean shave.

The men now, not only had to think about the 22 men left on Elephant Island, they also had to think about the crew of *Aurora* and the Ross Sea party. The men laying stores from the opposite side of Antarctica knew nothing about the sinking of *Endurance* and they carried on with their work of sledging long distances to leave stores at depots.

Over the next three months Tom Crean, Ernest Shackleton and Frank Worsley would try three times in three different ships to rescue the men on Elephant Island but each attempt failed because there was too much ice in the sea which blocked their path.

Finally on the fourth attempt, on board a ship called *Yelcho*, borrowed to them by Chile, a country in South America, they made it through the ice and Tom Crean and Ernest Shackleton picked up all 22 men in lifeboats and brought them back safely to the ship.

They sailed to a place called Punta Arenas in Chile where crowds had gathered to welcome them all home. As they left the ship, the *Yelcho's* captain, a man called Luis Pardo, his crew of Chilean sailors and all the crew of *Endurance*, were cheered on loudly by the crowds who knew how brave they all were.

The historic rescue was in newspapers all around the world and Tom Crean had once again shown great bravery. He'd played a most important part in saving the lives of his expedition friends.

In just four years between the *Terra Nova* expedition with Captain Scott and the *Endurance* expedition with Shackleton, Tom Crean had played a major role in saving the lives of 29 men.

Sadly, three men of the Ross Sea party who had continued their work to lay stores on the opposite side of Antarctica, were lost in bad weather conditions. Their ship *Aurora* had earlier been forced to sail to New Zealand after getting stuck in the ice but the ship,with Shackleton on board, returned to Antarctica to rescue the rest of the crew.

Tom returns home during the First World War

In November 1916 when Tom Crean returned home, the world was still in the middle of a war called the First World War.

There's a little bit of a mystery about why Tom was on a ship called the *HMS King Alfred* in Sierra Leone, a country in Africa in February 1917 but it could be that his help was needed to protect passenger ships from attack by German ships and submarines.

When Tom returned to Ireland he was based at a place called Berehaven which was a British Navy base in County Cork just 85 miles from his village of Annascaul so he didn't have far to go for short trips back home.

In September of 1917, Tom got married to a girl called Ellen and they had their wedding at the Sacred Heart Church in Annascaul.

Thinking about his life after finishing in the navy, Tom and Nell became publicans and his home was a place where people could meet to have a drink. It would later, in 1929, become known as the South Pole Inn and it's still a busy place in Annascaul today.

After he was married Tom had to return to work at Berehaven. The First World War was still being fought but in November 1918 the Germans

surrendered and the First World War came to an end.

Because the Germans had to surrender they also had to give up their warships. A fleet of British ships would escort them into a place called Scapa Flow, a huge British Navy base off the coast of Scotland. Tom Crean, by this time, had been made a Warrant Officer. It was a very important position to have reached and Tom must have been very proud of his achievement.

Tom was on a ship called *HMS Inflexible* which was among the ships following the defeated German ships into the bay at Scapa Flow. This was the final act of World War One and Tom would then leave the ship to join one called *HMS Fox*

Tom goes to Russia

In 1919, *HMS Fox* was sent to Russia as part of a huge international force.

Like the people of Ireland, the Russian people had never been happy with the way they were ruled and two years earlier, in 1917, a group called the Bolsheviks had taken over control of the country. They were known as the Reds and in what was called the Russian Civil War, they fought against their enemy who were known as the White Russians. Lots of countries decided to join together in what was called the North Russian Expeditionary Force. Their job was to go to Russia and try and stop the Bolsheviks from taking over more land as they marched forward.

Tom spent over seven months serving on *HMS Fox* and after people grew tired and angry of hearing about more deaths and injuries so soon after the First World War had ended, the Russian expeditionary force came home.

Throughout his life in the Navy, Tom had seen and had been at many places where people fought one another. He must have been really fed up with it.

It could be why he liked Antarctica so much. It was a place where everyone were friends.

Tom retires and returns home to Kerry

The last ship Tom would serve upon was called *HMS Hecla*.

In the year 1920, Tom Crean retired from the Navy after being in the Navy hospital for a month. The doctors said his eyesight wasn't good enough to continue as a sailor. His poorly eyes were probably caused by the blizzards and snowstorms he had faced in Antarctica.

It was around this time that he was asked once again to go on another expedition to Antarctica. Sir Ernest Shackleton was planning a fourth trip on a ship called *Quest* and he wanted Tom to go with him. For Tom though, there were more important things as he was now a husband and a father to very young children and he wanted to stay and look after them. Because of this he decided not to go back to Antarctica.

When he returned to Annascaul it was in the middle of another war called the Irish War of Independence. It was a war in which Irish people fought to be free to rule their own country and it was fought against the British who still ruled Ireland. There was a really cruel group of people sent to Ireland by the British called the Black and Tans.

They carried out nasty, horrible things against the Irish people.

One day the Black and Tans rushed into Tom's home because they knew he was a person who wanted Ireland to be a free country. They were looking for proof of this when they found papers showing he had been in the British Navy. Because of this, they called off the search and they left.

Tom had always been a proud Irishman who loved his country. On his first expedition to Antarctica he had a little Irish flag tied to his sledge.

The War of Independence saw many lives lost and one of these was his older brother, Cornelius. He was a policeman who was shot in County Cork where he worked. It was really sad news for Tom and his family. He travelled with his brother Daniel and their youngest sister, Catherine, to be at their brother's funeral.

After the Irish War of Independence there was another war called the Irish Civil War and after it was over it later led to Ireland ruling it's own country called the Republic of Ireland

Tom lived the rest of his life in Annascaul

Tom and his wife Ellen had three daughters, Mary, Kate and Eileen. Kate, the middle of his three daughters, was a sick child and she died very young in 1924, aged just three years old. It was heartbreaking for Tom and his wife losing their little girl and it happened just two months after Tom's mother had passed away.

Tom didn't spend so much time in the pub and it

was his wife Nell who looked after the customers when they came in for a drink and a chat.

Most evenings he would go for a walk and would always take his two dogs who were called Fido and Toby. Tom had always loved animals and going for a stroll with him most evenings would be his young godson, John Knightly. John was the son of Tom's best friend in Annascaul, Robert Knightly, the train station master.

John remembered one night as they walked the dogs down to a nearby beach called Bunaneer, that one of the dogs fell off a hillside and onto the beach below. Tom and young John rushed down but they couldn't save the poor dog. John remembered how Tom was so upset at the loss of his beloved dog, he stood over it and cried.

Funny Crean

Tom Crean was a mighty man and not just because of the lives he saved. He was mighty in many other ways. He made people feel better when they were feeling down. He made people laugh, he was a good and kind friend to his neighbours and children loved being in his company. The children of Annascaul knew him as 'Funny Crean' and his godson John remembers that his mother would lock the door if she saw Tom coming to the house in the evening because she knew she'd never get her children to sleep if Tom came in and had them in fits of laughter.

One of the funniest stories about Tom happened when a group of men called into the pub one Friday morning when the train to Dingle had broken down near Annascaul. The men were on their way to the fair for the weekend. With them the men had brought a few bites to eat for the weekend. They called in to Tom's place because they knew there was a big kitchen there and sure enough Tom took a few sausages and bacon slices from the men and began frying them up in the pan. Soon, the lovely smell of the breakfast filled the place and had reached Tom's wife Nell who was upstairs.

Both Tom and his wife went to church regularly on a Sunday and at this time being good Catholics meant that no-one was allowed to eat any meat on a Friday. This was one time that Tom had forgotten what day it was and he carried on frying the breakfast to feed the hungry men waiting for it to be served.

As Nell caught the smell of the food, she set about Tom for breaking the holy rules and she shouted down at him: *"Tom Crean"* she said, *"What the heck do you think you're doing frying sausages on Friday, a Holy Day when we can't be eating meat?"*

Tom, by now busy putting the food on the plates shouted back up: *"If you'd been in Antarctica where I'd spent many a Friday starving, I'd have eaten a slice of meat off your bottom"* The men, tucking into their food, laughed at Tom's reply but we can be sure Tom's wife didn't.

His travels had taken him many thousands of miles and he walked more miles on Antarctica than both Captain Scott and Sir Ernest Shackleton, the two leaders he'd served with. His long treks over the snow and ice had an effect on his poor feet and suffering many times from frostbite had left them sore with dark patches. After he retired his feet caused him so much pain that he had to have boots specially made for him because normal shoes would cause him too much pain. To help ease the pain Tom would sometimes take off his shoes and dip his feet into the river that ran next to his pub.

Two local children remembered seeing the poor feet of their friend 'Funny Crean' one day as he washed them. Tom was glad it was only the children who had seen his feet as he didn't want to talk about how they became so sore after walking over thousands of miles of snow and ice. Although Tom saved many lives he had also lost many friends in Antarctica and it had left him with a lot of sad memories.

Tom becomes ill and passes away

When Tom reached the age of 61, he became ill and had bad pains in his tummy. The nearest hospital was in a town called Tralee and he was taken there so the doctors could see what was wrong with him.

At the hospital they found out that Tom was suffering from an illness that lots of people normally get better from after a small operation. The trouble was that there was no doctor in Tralee who was able to do the operation.

This was really bad news because waiting meant that his condition could only become worse and this meant that his life would be in danger.

Tom had to travel to a hospital in Cork which was over 70 miles away. It was the nearest hospital in which there was a doctor able to operate on him.

Tom finally had the operation but it was too late as his stomach had already become much worse after having waited too long.

Tom never got better and he died on 27th July 1938.

It was so sad to think that the mighty explorer who had saved so many lives had no one there to save his life when he needed help.

He was brought back to Annascaul where his funeral took place the following day.

After a mass at the Sacred Heart Church in Annascaul where he had been baptised and married, his coffin was laid to rest in a stone tomb he built himself. Tom's final resting place was in a graveyard at Ballynacourty, close to Gortacurraun where he was born.

The crowd at his funeral was the biggest Annascaul had ever seen and on the top of his tomb lay a glass bowl with porcelain flowers inside. It was sent by Teddy Evans whose life he had saved in Antarctica.

Evans, who at the time of Tom's death had reached the highest position of Admiral in the Royal Navy, always remembered the bravery of Tom Crean in walking 35 miles through freezing blizzards to save his life and the note with the

glass bowl read: *'In fond remembrance of an Antarctic comrade'*

Today, people from all over the world come to Annascaul and visit Tom's pub, the South Pole Inn where lots of pictures of Tom are hung on the walls. People also visit the graveyard where Tom is buried which is not far from the village.

As more and more people find out about his story, he becomes a hero to new fans from all over the world.

There are a huge number of people living across the world today who are the children, grandchildren or are in some way related to the men that Tom saved.

I wonder if they know they only exist because of the bravery of Tom The Mighty Explorer?

Maps of Tom's Journeys

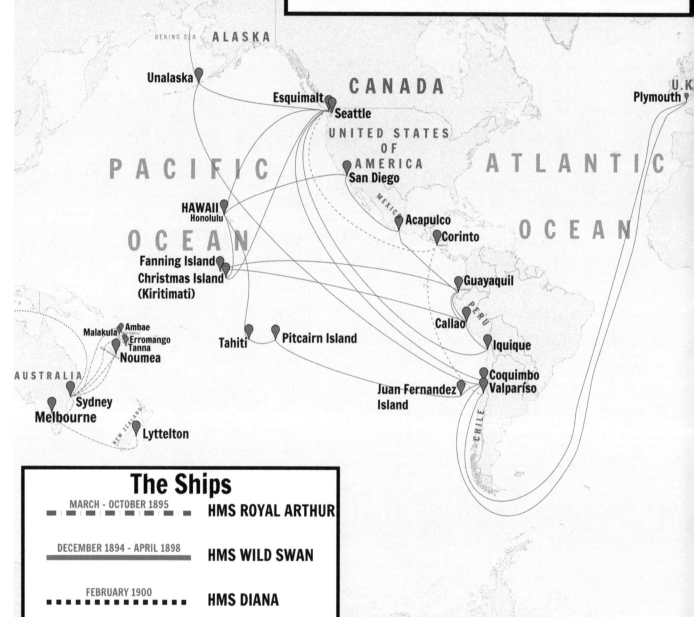

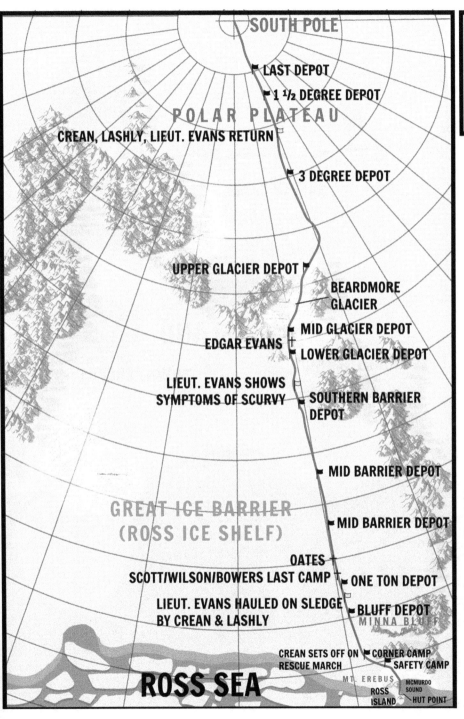

SOUTH POLE

LAST DEPOT

1 ½ DEGREE DEPOT

POLAR PLATEAU

CREAN, LASHLY, LIEUT. EVANS RETURN

3 DEGREE DEPOT

UPPER GLACIER DEPOT

BEARDMORE GLACIER

MID GLACIER DEPOT

EDGAR EVANS

LOWER GLACIER DEPOT

LIEUT. EVANS SHOWS SYMPTOMS OF SCURVY

SOUTHERN BARRIER DEPOT

MID BARRIER DEPOT

GREAT ICE BARRIER (ROSS ICE SHELF)

MID BARRIER DEPOT

OATES

SCOTT/WILSON/BOWERS LAST CAMP

ONE TON DEPOT

LIEUT. EVANS HAULED ON SLEDGE BY CREAN & LASHLY

BLUFF DEPOT

MINNA BLUFF

CREAN SETS OFF ON RESCUE MARCH

CORNER CAMP

SAFETY CAMP

MT. EREBUS

ROSS SEA

ROSS ISLAND

MCMURDO SOUND

HUT POINT

Tom's Journey with Scott

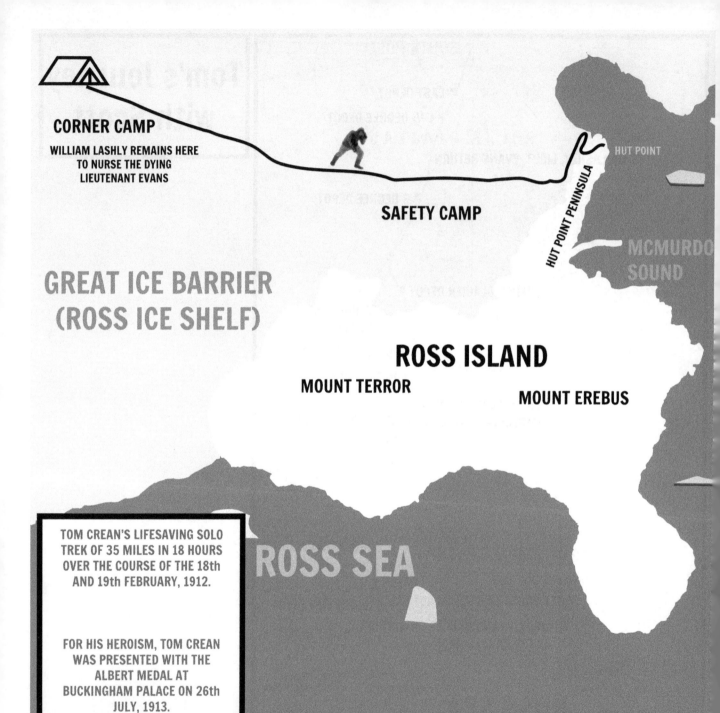

CORNER CAMP

WILLIAM LASHLY REMAINS HERE
TO NURSE THE DYING
LIEUTENANT EVANS

SAFETY CAMP

HUT POINT

HUT POINT PENINSULA

MCMURDO
SOUND

GREAT ICE BARRIER
(ROSS ICE SHELF)

ROSS ISLAND

MOUNT TERROR

MOUNT EREBUS

ROSS SEA

TOM CREAN'S LIFESAVING SOLO
TREK OF 35 MILES IN 18 HOURS
OVER THE COURSE OF THE 18th
AND 19th FEBRUARY, 1912.

FOR HIS HEROISM, TOM CREAN
WAS PRESENTED WITH THE
ALBERT MEDAL AT
BUCKINGHAM PALACE ON 26th
JULY, 1913.

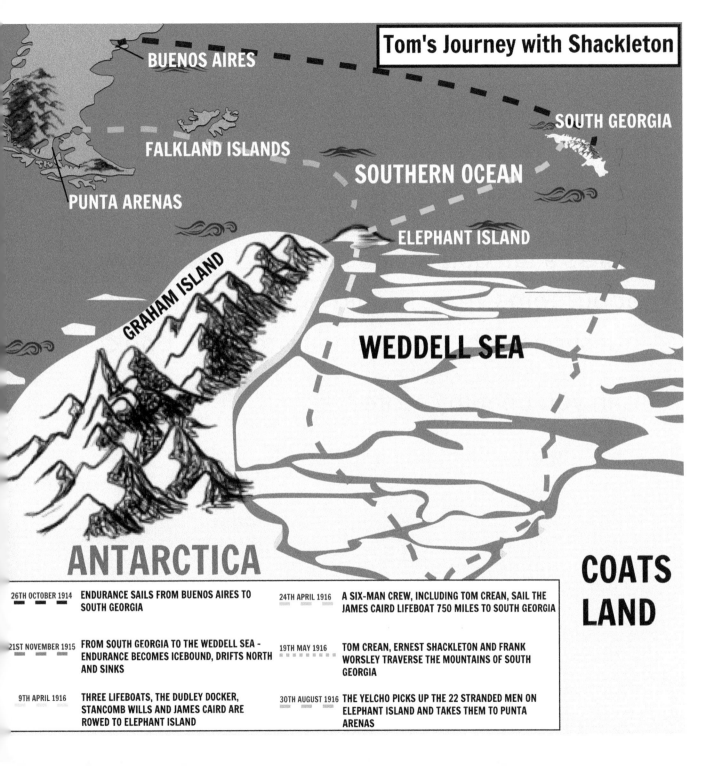

Tom's Journey with Shackleton

BUENOS AIRES

SOUTH GEORGIA

FALKLAND ISLANDS

SOUTHERN OCEAN

PUNTA ARENAS

ELEPHANT ISLAND

GRAHAM ISLAND

WEDDELL SEA

ANTARCTICA

COATS LAND

26TH OCTOBER 1914 — ENDURANCE SAILS FROM BUENOS AIRES TO SOUTH GEORGIA

21ST NOVEMBER 1915 — FROM SOUTH GEORGIA TO THE WEDDELL SEA - ENDURANCE BECOMES ICEBOUND, DRIFTS NORTH AND SINKS

9TH APRIL 1916 — THREE LIFEBOATS, THE DUDLEY DOCKER, STANCOMB WILLS AND JAMES CAIRD ARE ROWED TO ELEPHANT ISLAND

24TH APRIL 1916 — A SIX-MAN CREW, INCLUDING TOM CREAN, SAIL THE JAMES CAIRD LIFEBOAT 750 MILES TO SOUTH GEORGIA

19TH MAY 1916 — TOM CREAN, ERNEST SHACKLETON AND FRANK WORSLEY TRAVERSE THE MOUNTAINS OF SOUTH GEORGIA

30TH AUGUST 1916 — THE YELCHO PICKS UP THE 22 STRANDED MEN ON ELEPHANT ISLAND AND TAKES THEM TO PUNTA ARENAS

The Ten Question Tom Quiz

Here's a fun quiz to see how much you know about Tom Crean. I could only get 5 of the questions right myself and I wrote the book.

Can you beat my score?

1. Tom Crean was a really proud Irish person but do you know where in Ireland he was born?

> Belfast
>
> Dublin
>
> Annascaul

2. He was an explorer who went on three journeys to help find out more about the place he visited. Do you know which part of the world this was?

> China
>
> Antarctica
>
> Russia

3. Tom was a really brave person who saved lots of other people's lives. For saving the life of Edward Evans he walked 35 miles in the snow and wind on his own. He was given a medal for this. What was the name of the medal?

> The Albert Medal
> The Michael Medal
> The Margaret Medal

4. Tom Crean was almost 16 and a half years old when he joined the Navy and his first expedition was with Captain Scott in the year 1901, over a hundred years ago. Do you know the name of the ship they sailed on?

> Discovery
> The Good Ship Lollipop
> The Starship Enterprise

5. Tom Crean was born in the year 1877 which was a time when times were hard and people were extremely poor. Do you know the date of his birthday?

> 16th February
> 25th October
> 12th March

6. On Tom's second expedition Captain Scott wanted to be the first person to reach a certain place where no person had ever been before. What was the place called?

> Mount Everest
> The South Pole
> The North Pole

7. His last expedition to Antarctica was on a ship called Endurance and the leader was another Irishman. Do you know who this person was?

Sir Michael Shufflebottom

Sir Ernest Shackleton

Sir Henry Stinkyboots

8. Tom Crean came from a big family. Do you know how many brothers and sisters he had?

8 brothers and 2 sisters

1 brother and 10 sisters

7 brothers and 3 sisters

9. Captain Scott didn't choose Tom Crean to be in his final party and he had to return across the ice back to the expedition hut with two other people. What were they called?

Lieutenant Pigeon and Willy Wonka

Lieutenant Evans and William Lashly

Lieutenant Lashly and William Evans

10. Which football team do you think Tom Crean supported?

Kerry

Dublin

Galway

On the opposite page tell us why you think Tom Crean is a hero to children. There are no right or wrong answers for this but it would be really good to read why you like Tom.

Written by _____ On the_____

That Doesn't Belong In Antarctica

In the picture of Antarctica opposite there are six things that shouldn't be there. Can you tell us what they are?

All Named After Tom Crean

Crean Lake in South Georgia

Crean Glacier in South Georgia

Mount Crean in Antarctica

Mount Crean in Greenland

Crean Deep a massive underwater trench close to New Zealand

There's even a meteorite named after Tom. It's called Crean 01400 and it was discovered on Mount Crean in Antarctica by a team of scientists in 2001.

'I hope that you enjoyed the story
all about Tom Crean
The bravest of explorers the world
has ever seen
And if one day Antarctica's the
place you'd like to go
Don't forget to wrap up warm
To keep out all the snow'

If you'd like to get in touch with me or have
any questions about Tom this is my email
address timfoley50@googlemail.com

Not The End Because…

There's a grown-ups book I wrote about Tom that you might want to read when you're a little older.

There's lots about that and Tom at this website www.tomcreanbook.com

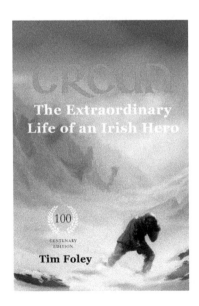

There's a grown-ups book I wrote about Tom that
you might want to read when you're a little older.

There's lots about that and Tom at this website

www.tomgreenbook.com